CAS:
RODEO
COWGIRL

Laura B. Edge

Illustrated by Stephanie Ford

PELICAN PUBLISHING COMPANY
GRETNA 2017

ISBN: 9781455622771
E-book ISBN: 9781455622788

Printed in China

Published by Pelican Publishing Company, Inc.
1000 Burmaster Street, Gretna, Louisiana 70053

For Gerry, my cowboy, best friend, cheerleader, and
soul mate —LBE

To my mom and dad, for all the early mornings, late
nights, and hours spent sitting in the cold and heat by
the side of a riding arena, and for all that you gave to
raise a horse-crazy girl. Thank you. —SF

Tad and her brothers saddled their horses. They rode to the Gordon, Nebraska, county fair. It was quite a spectacle!

They saw farm wagons piled high with watermelon, squash, beets, and pumpkins. Long tables overflowed with flowers and fruit. Homemade quilts, draped over clothes lines, fluttered in the breeze.

Cowboys herded the finest horses, sheep, hogs, and cattle into corrals. Mamas chased their dusty children as they ran laughing through the crowds. It seemed like all of Nebraska had come out to join the fun at the fair.

Fourteen-year-old Tad was there on official business. Her neighbor had asked her to ride his horse in a race. Tad loved to ride. The faster the better!

After the race, Tad met Mildred, a bronc-riding cowgirl. Mildred wanted to ride a steer at the fair. Steer riding was a man's event, but Mildred pestered the judges until, at last, they agreed. Tad decided to ride a steer too and make a contest out of it.

Mildred rode first. The wild steer kicked and spun. He stomped and snorted and spun some more.

Mildred landed with a whump on the hard ground.
She picked up her cowboy hat, waved to the crowd,
and trotted out of the arena.

Tad was next. If she could stay on her steer until the buzzer sounded, she would win the contest.

She climbed aboard, and the beast took off.

The steer humped his back and ducked his head between his legs. Then he spun and bucked in tight circles.

The crowd whooped and hollered.

"Yee-ha!" yelled Tad.

The buzzer screeched. Tad won the contest and the twenty-five dollar prize!

"Riding is a fine way to make a living," she told her brother.

Tad was born Barbara Barnes in Cody, Nebraska, on September 1, 1902, the youngest of twenty-four children. She didn't crawl like most babies; she slithered. Her dad thought she looked like a tadpole. The name stuck, and everyone called her "Tad." She learned to ride almost before she could walk. "I can't remember when I didn't ride," she said.

By the time she was seven, she was helping her dad tame wild horses.

Rodeo cowgirls learned their sport in an actual working occupation: cattle ranching.

Tad rode her coal-black horse three miles to school each day. On the way, she raced her brothers and sisters, her friends, and the Sioux Indians who lived nearby.

Her family moved to Fort Worth, Texas, and Tad fell in love with the Lone Star State. She competed in small rodeos in tiny Texas towns. Then she moved on to bigger and bigger contests. She'd load her horse on a special train car and sew her costumes on the way.

She made costumes of whipcord, a strong braided fabric. She also made velvet suits with rhinestone trim. When she rode broncs, she wore wooly Angora chaps. "If we had to ride a bull or a bucking horse or anything else, we wore our best clothes," she said.

Tad performed in rodeos all across the United States and Mexico. At big-city rodeos, she stayed in hotels. When she traveled in the summertime, she slept in a tent. She rode bucking horses, or broncs, and ornery bulls. She also raced other cowgirls.

In relay races, Tad circled the track four times. She changed horses after each lap. Her feet never touched the ground as she leapt from one running horse to another. At the Pendleton Round-Up, Tad left her first horse and grabbed on to her next mount's saddle horn. Stretched out between two running horses, her foot caught in the stirrup. With a swift kick, she managed to free her foot, gain her seat on the second horse, and win the race.

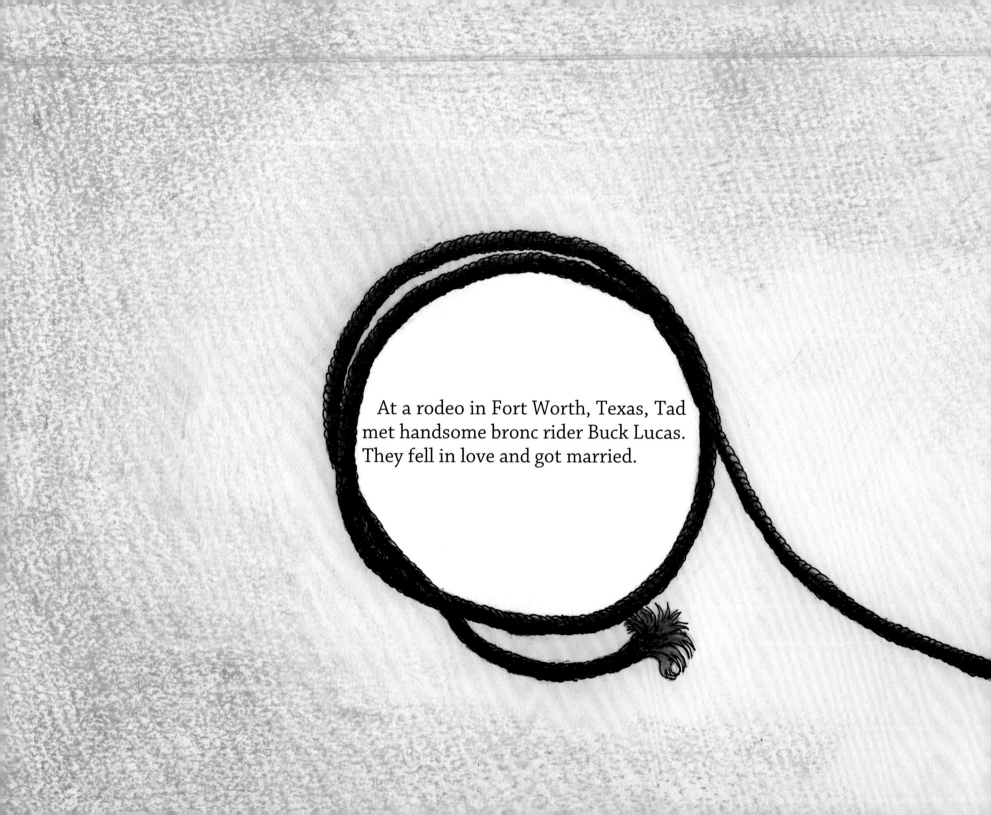

At a rodeo in Fort Worth, Texas, Tad met handsome bronc rider Buck Lucas. They fell in love and got married.

Tad and Buck spent their honey-moon on a ship to England with the Tex Austin Wild West Show. At the rodeo in England, Tad amazed the crowd by doing tricks on her horse. The audience loved the tiny daredevil.

After that, trick riding became Tad's specialty.

Trick riders were judged on the difficulty of their tricks and how well they did them. The horse was judged on how fast he ran.

Tad did tricks other riders wouldn't try and made them look easy. At the Madison Square Garden rodeo in New York City, she stood on her saddle while her horse raced around the arena. She stood on her head, supporting her weight by holding onto leather straps.

Tad won the trick-riding contest at the Madison Square Garden rodeo eight times. She also won the champion all-around cowgirl award three times in a row.

She held on to the saddle horn and cartwheeled along the side of her horse.

Tad won the hearts of the crowd and the trophy when she leaned over the back of her horse. Her head was just inches from his pounding hooves.

Tad and Buck bought a ranch in Fort Worth, Texas, and had two daughters. They built a practice arena where Tad could try out new rodeo tricks. She liked to practice by moonlight, when her girls were asleep.

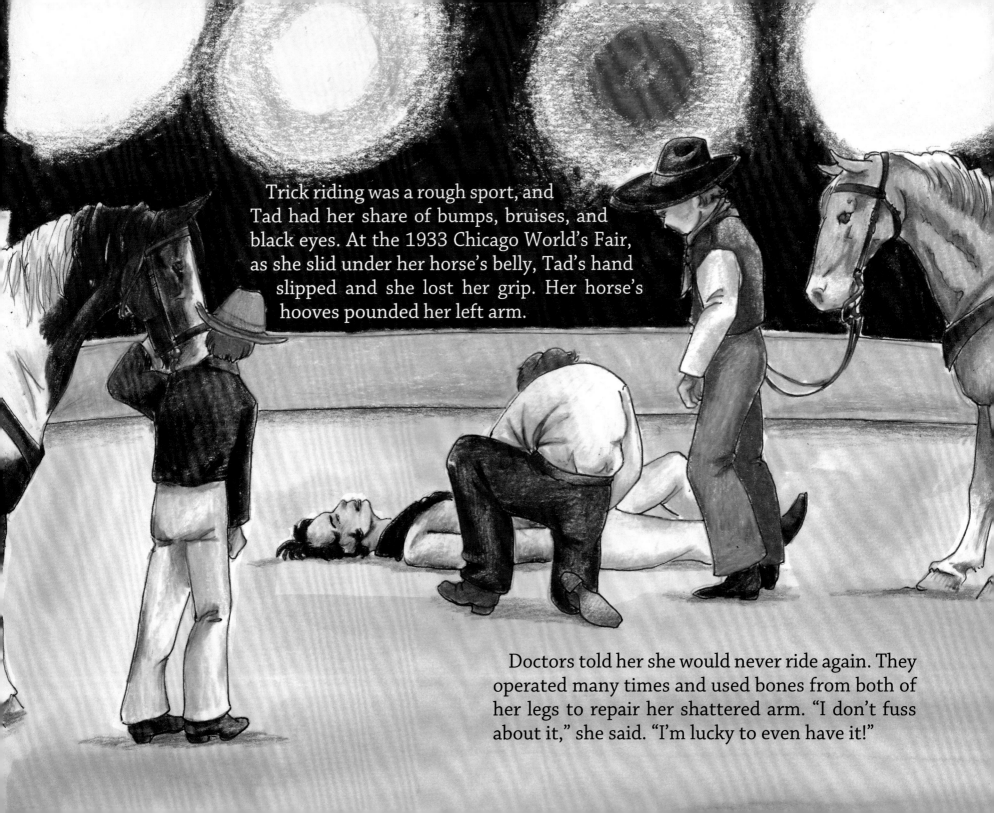

Trick riding was a rough sport, and Tad had her share of bumps, bruises, and black eyes. At the 1933 Chicago World's Fair, as she slid under her horse's belly, Tad's hand slipped and she lost her grip. Her horse's hooves pounded her left arm.

Doctors told her she would never ride again. They operated many times and used bones from both of her legs to repair her shattered arm. "I don't fuss about it," she said. "I'm lucky to even have it!"

Tad wore a heavy cast for three years, but that didn't slow her down. She was back in the saddle trick riding in a year. She learned tricks she could do with one arm in a cast. Mitzi, Tad's five-year-old daughter, performed with her. Tad did some tricks, Mitzi did some tricks, and the crowd cheered.

During World War II, women's events were dropped from rodeos. Tad helped start the Women's Professional Rodeo Association to give girls a chance to compete.

Tad and Mitzi did trick-riding routines together for twenty years. Tad also rode broncs after her accident, holding on with her right hand instead of her left. She performed until she was fifty-six years old and won trophies from hundreds of rodeos in trick riding, bronc riding, and relay racing.

Tad Lucas has been called Rodeo's First Lady and the greatest cowgirl of all time. She is the only cowgirl honored by all three rodeo halls of fame: the National Rodeo Hall of Fame, the National Cowgirl Hall of Fame, and the ProRodeo Hall of Fame.

METRO
GOLDWVN
MAYER
CHAPP.
T.

Tad died in 1990. In her will, she left plans for an award to honor women who excel in any field related to Western heritage. Her daughter Mitzi established the Tad Lucas Memorial Award to fulfill her mother's wishes. Tad showed that women could hold jobs once thought of as only for men. She proved they were the equal of men in guts, daring, and bravery. Her spirit lives on in any girl who follows her heart and dares to be different.

AUTHOR'S NOTE

In the early 1900s, women were considered fragile, delicate, and practically helpless. They wore tight corsets under floor-length dresses and rode sidesaddle. Cowgirls introduced split skirts, so they could ride astride. But split skirts weren't considered respectable. When a cowgirl in Montana rode into town in one, the sheriff threatened to arrest her!

Women had limited career options. They could hold jobs as teachers, factory workers, or domestic servants. Tad Lucas and her fellow cowgirls played a large part in changing those stereotypes. Rodeos and Wild West shows provided a good way for women to earn a living. They could earn more money competing in rodeos than they could at traditional jobs. These spunky cowgirls proved that women were strong, smart, and capable. Because of them, girls today can choose to be astronauts or presidents, police officers or soldiers. Like Tad, they can follow their dreams.

Tad and her daughter Mitzi (National Cowgirl Museum and Hall of Fame, Fort Worth, Texas)